AF330099

DESTINATION *Victoria*

MAGNIFICENT PANORAMIC VIEWS

Born and raised on the Murray River, Ken Duncan has long enjoyed a special relationship with Australia's south-east corner. Even today, as a critically acclaimed photographer travelling the globe, Ken loves to return to the region he considers one of the most picturesque and diverse on earth. As host state for the Melbourne 2006 Commonwealth Games, Victoria is now attracting renewed interest from people

all over the world. Its natural magnificence is reflected in the colours chosen for the official Games logo: Blue for the state's dramatic coastline, green for its lush vegetation, red, orange and yellow for the sun's ever-changing glow.

From its haunting high country to its hidden beaches, Victoria's beauty is wonderfully displayed in this delightful collection of Ken Duncan landscapes.

JAMES MATTHEW BARRIE

*Those who bring
sunshine to the lives
of others cannot keep it
from themselves.*

TITLE PAGE
Face of the Ages, The Twelve Apostles

PREVIOUS PAGE
Fern Gully, Young Creek, Otway State Forest

THIS PAGE
Refuge Cove, Wilsons Promontory

Adversity
is the cauldron
in which
character is formed.

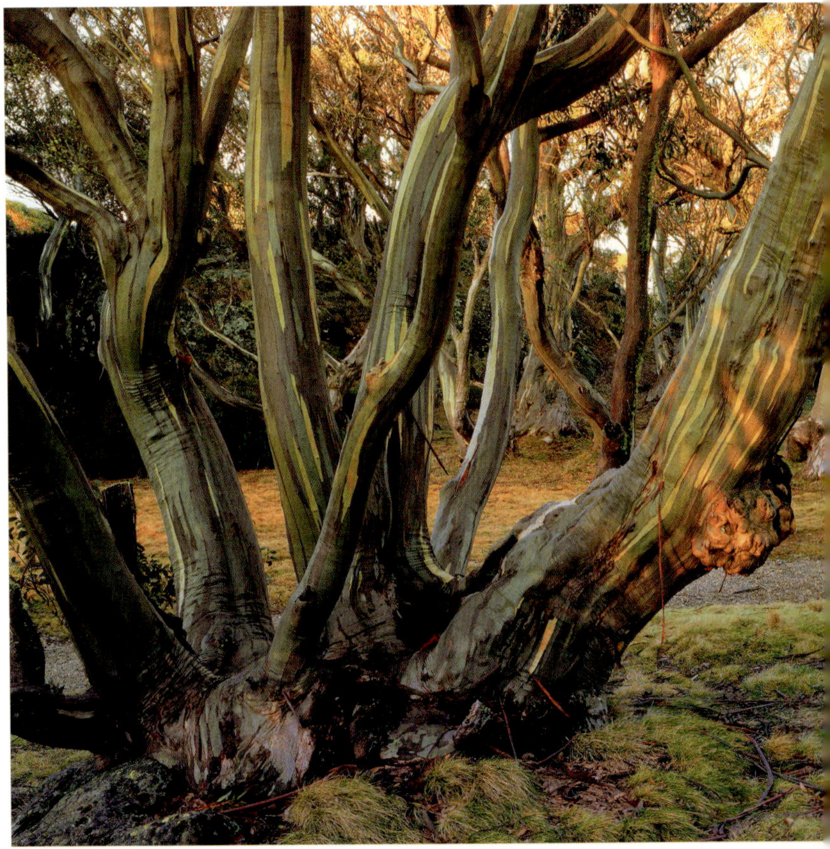

THIS PAGE
Wallace Hut, Falls Creek

NEXT PAGE
Country Garden, Mirranatwa, Serra Ranges

*Kind words can be
short and easy to speak,
but their echoes
are truly endless.*

Hopetoun Falls, Otway State Forest

Happiness is a perfume
you cannot pour on others
without getting
a few drops on yourself.

THIS PAGE
Sunrise, Johanna Beach

NEXT PAGE
Southern Dreaming, The Twelve Apostles

Nothing ever becomes real till it is experienced.

Valley mist, Omeo Valley

*No man fails
who does his best...*

THIS PAGE
Craig's Hut, Alpine National Park

NEXT PAGE
Majestic Melbourne

BASIL S. WALSH

If you don't know where you are going, how can you expect to get there?

Puffing Billy, The Dandenongs

CLEARANCE
4.5m

BOOT MAKER
CORDIAL LEMONADE
Dr CARR
BOWLING ALLEY

GEORGE MOORE

After all,
there is but one race;
humanity.

THIS PAGE
Re-enactment of the Eureka Rebellion 1854,
Sovereign Hill, Ballarat

NEXT PAGE
Majestic sunset, Mansfield

*In the middle
of difficulty
lies opportunity.*

PREVIOUS PAGE
Misty morning, Strzelecki Ranges

THIS PAGE
Murray River reflections

31

Laughter is the sun
that drives winter
from the human face.

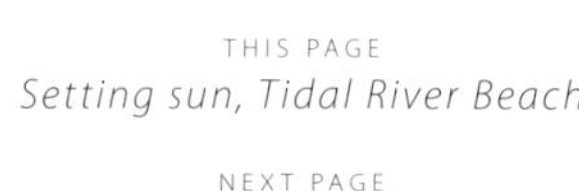

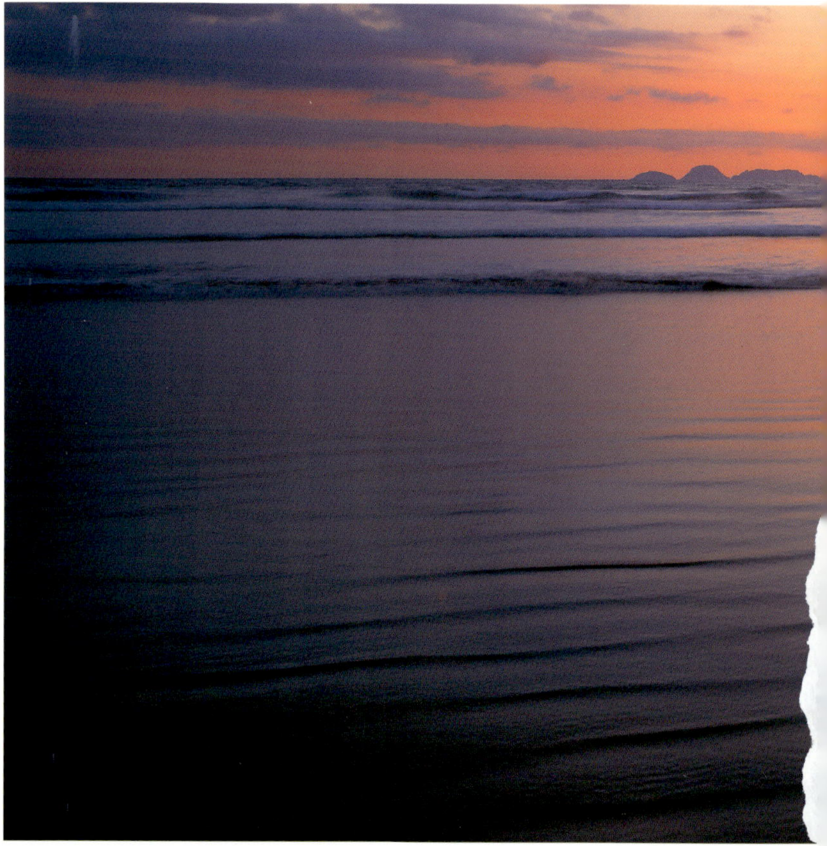

THIS PAGE
Setting sun, Tidal River Beach

NEXT PAGE
Rolling Hills, Johanna

*The secret of success
is constancy of purpose.*

PREVIOUS PAGE
Snowy River gums, Alpine National Park

THIS PAGE
Mackenzie Falls, Grampians National Park

*A man
without a purpose
is like a ship
without a rudder.*

*Peace starts
with you and me.*

Sunrise, Shipwreck Creek, Croajingalong National Park

DESTINATION VICTORIA
First published 2005
by Panographs® Publishing Pty Ltd
ABN 21 050 235 606
PO Box 3015, Wamberal,
NSW, 2260, Australia
Telephone +61 2 4367 6777
Email: panos@kenduncan.com

The National Library of Australia
Cataloguing-in-Publication entry:
Duncan, Ken
Destination Victoria:
magnificent panoramic views.
ISBN 0 9751775 3 2
1. Victoria - Pictorial works. I. Title.
919.4500222
To view the range of Ken Duncan's
panoramic Limited Edition Prints
visit our Galleries:

- **5740 Oak Road, Matcham, NSW**
  Telephone +61 2 4367 6701
- **73 George Street, The Rocks,**
  Sydney, NSW
  Telephone +61 2 9241 3460
- **Shop U6 Southgate,**
  Melbourne, Vic
  Telephone +61 3 9686 8022
- **Shop 14 Hunter Valley**
  Gardens Village,
  Broke Road, Pokolbin, NSW
  Telephone +61 2 4998 6711